LORENZ TARAH

SELF-PUBLISHING

**The Ultimate Guide On How to Self-Publish a Book,
Learn the Easiest and Most Effective Ways on How You Can Publish
Your Book Without a Traditional Publisher**

Descrierea CIP a Bibliotecii Naţionale a României
LORENZ TARAH
   SELF-PUBLISHING. The Ultimate Guide On How to Self-Publish a Book, Learn the Easiest and Most Effective Ways on How You Can Publish Your Book Without a Traditional Publisher / Lorenz Tarah – Bucharest: Editura My Ebook, 2021
   ISBN

LORENZ TARAH

SELF-PUBLISHING

**The Ultimate Guide On How to Self-Publish a Book,
Learn the Easiest and Most Effective Ways on How You
Can Publish Your Book Without a Traditional Publisher**

My Ebook Publishing House
Bucharest, 2021

TABLE OF CONTENTS

INTRODUCTION

Presidential Medal of Freedom winner and acclaimed American author Toni Morrison once said: "If there's a book that you want to read, but it hasn't been written yet, then you must write it."

Good advice – especially in this day and age, where traditional publishing is only one of the options you can choose, when it comes to making sure others read your books. And, according to many mainstream sources, it may not even be your best option. (Think about it: Even assuming it's going to be accepted by a traditional publisher, not only are publishers getting pickier and pickier (and turning out less titles) but there will be at least a year in between submitting your manuscript, having it reviewed, then sent to a higher authority, then accepted, then negotiated. And *then* production begins...)

This comprehensive guide will present you with a variety of self-publishing options and explore their viability. We'll take a look at all types of books and book-delivery systems, including:

- Information Products

- Kindle eBooks

- Books on CD/DVD

- Audio books (DC and MP3)

- Hardcover books

- Pictorial books (Manga, comics, photo books, calendars)

We will finish off (almost) with CreateSpace, Amazon's own self-publishing machine – one of the most popular self-publishing venues today. Before you rush to sign up with CreateSpace (which does have some noticeable disadvantages, to be weighed against its very real advantages) or join the Kindle eBook bandwagon, do take time to check out your alternatives.

After all, ***ninety-per cent of self-publishing success*** lies in taking time to plan your publishing strategy and putting yourself in a position to make the right informed choice.

Make no mistake: Self-publishing the easy way involves:

- Knowing your market – and their reading method preferences

- Determining your budget

- Determining what elements are essential for your target reader… and what you can live without

- Picking the right company

- Having an overall goal and plan

- Being prepared to create a marketing and promotion plan for your book and putting it into action

Traditional Publishing Vs. Self-publishing

There are usually two major reasons people select self-publishing, when it comes to getting their books out there:

1. **The book has been rejected by a slew of traditional publishing houses**, and the author is considering self-publishing out of frustration and a strong belief in their book/message.

2. **To make money fast**. In the shortest time possible.

If you lean towards the latter motivation, your strategies will need to be very different from someone who has written what they believe to be the Greatest Literary Masterpiece of all time – those are usually dependent on getting reviewed by the right authority sources.

Your strategies will also be affected by budget and your value system.

If making fast money is your primary concern and your venue is sales, you would almost certainly want to choose creating a Kindle eBook over approaching a publisher. On the other hand, if you've written the great existential novel of our time, your best course to reputation-building and review potential might be to approach the right traditional publishing house and cultivating literary magazine editors and reviewers. In other words, everything is relative: There's no "one size fits all" for self-publishing.

Before we start looking at self-publishing options, however, let's focus on the one essential "law" you must observe and obey…

The Forty-Seventh Principle

Whichever way you choose to go, you'll also need to make sure your visionary book-publishing plan includes this vital component:

- **A unique story angle**, slanted at **the right market**

Approach it this way, visually, using your imagination…

Think of yourself as an editor at a top publishing house: Forty-six manuscripts land on your desk. They are all about the importance of creating a Facebook Page. Each one starts off with a bunch of statistics on Facebook usage, does a little Rah-Rah dance for Facebook's "potential"; then walks the reader through setting up a Facebook Page. Trouble is, you're looking for a book that will convince the Post-Graduate degree-heavy LinkedIn market that Facebook is worth considering. They want information about it but they want more than a "how to" or superficial hype.

This audience really wants to understand *what makes people tick*: And *why* they choose Facebook over all other social networks.

Enter the forty-seventh Facebook author. She presents you with a dynamic, crystal-clear outline for her proposed book, "The Universal Playground"[1]. In it, she explores how Facebook alters the communication dynamics of people on a psychological level, showing why it makes them reveal intimate details they would never divulge in a million years if face-to-face with strangers.

Instantly, you (as Publisher) feel excitement flooding your veins. You're quivering like a downhill ski-jumper about to launch herself down the 570-meter take-off ramp at Vikersundbakken during the FIS ski-flying championships.

Instantly, you envision the book cover for "The Universal Playground": A group of adults solemnly playing in a children's playground, dressed in outfits from all walks of life. You find yourself deciding which photographer to use before you've even finished reading the rest of the Author's short but well-crafted query letter.

---

[1] You're instantly captivated by the snappy Title, of course.

But wait: Get a check on your emotions. *Keeping in mind your super- educated LinkedIn audience,* which book out of the forty-seven proposals would you, as publisher, choose? You have to put aside your own love for "The Universal Playground" for a moment and think which one would be the most **lucrative** prospect in the long run.

That's right: The book that is…

- Most accurately written for and slanted to your specific, desired audience
- With a catchy title (again, slanted directly at your desired audience's educational level and interests)

- That addresses the issues your audience is hungry to answer
- That excites you to the point of envisioning covers and quivering with adrenalin
- That is unique

It stands out from the herd. By miles.

The Excitement Factor

You don't have to write a New York Best-seller or win the Pulitzer Prize, like Toni Morrison. But your book should excite you as much as it should excite any third-party Publisher. You should feel so "in the zone" about your book idea, your adrenalin starts pumping and you are envisioning promotional tactics, chapter beginnings, alternate endings, television appearances...

But your job is tougher. A third-party publisher (i.e. editor, most likely) has zero emotional attachment to any of the book ideas that cross her desk... and possibly a much stronger, more familiar and sharper grasp on who her audience is. You are blinded by emotional attachment, love of your subject; enamored of your own brilliant idea and convinced it is worth it because you poured so much time and passion into it.

That's when, as Self-Publisher, you have to step back after that initial excitement and ask yourself the tough but essential questions:

- "Have people been waiting for this book?"

- "Is it suited to the target audience I have in mind?"

- "Is it saying something unique and different to all other books on this subject?"

- "What is the `extra twist' that makes it transcend all other books on the subject?"

- "Does my audience really need – or want – this book?"

- "Will it entertain, touch and excite them? Will it make their lives better... or help them defeat an obstacle that's been confounding them for ages?"

- "Does it speak for everyone? Is the theme universal?"

And THEN you have to ask yourself that penultimate Publisher's question - the one that has literally seen Editors sobbing with disappointment as they are reluctantly forced to reject the best book they've ever seen written[1]...

---

[1] Don't worry. This rarely ever happens in the Publishing world. Alas.

- *how much money will it make us? Is it worth our investment?*

And now you know how a "real" Publisher/editor works.

That is exactly how you have to approach your Self-publishing project, if you want to experience even a measure of success.

But wait… just one more teensy-weensy point, before we get down-an'- dirty with the various Self-publishing methods waiting for your pocketbook.

And that's the other vital element, besides writing a unique, relevant book whose time has come…

- **A strong marketing and promotion plan**, aimed at the right audience and lasting long enough to build up buzz

Marketing and Promotion

"But can't I just leave that up to the publishing house I picked?", you quaver. "It says here in the fine print they'll take care of all that stuff..."

One of the biggest drawbacks to self-publishing – traditionally and currently – has always been the area of marketing and promotion. Typically, "vanity presses" take a whack of money from you, promise to place your book in various markets and promote it. Let's make a long story shorter than the shortest violin in the world (playing just for you, if you fall victim to this "we'll make it easy" scamming) and say that... it doesn't usually happen that way.

It's like link-farming. A spurious SEO company takes your money, promises you thirty-thousand backlinks on top-rated sites... then does this by planting viruses containing your link within unknowing, legitimate sites' HTML... along with links to casinos, porn sites and other Google-loathed shady customers.

Not doing your homework leaves you wide open to that sort of exploitation. No matter what "they" promise.

If you don't believe me, just take a quick look at top-selling authors. All but the most famous frequently still do "book tours" and appear on TV talk shows and local radio, tirelessly promoting their books. They'll blog.

They'll have a social media presence. They'll hire publicists who make sure the right magazines and newspapers receive juicy press releases about their private lives (right when the new book is coming out).

The fact is… unless you're a Stephen King or a J. K. Rowling (in which case you'll hire a full-time security service to chase paparazzi *away* every time you step out of your door) you are going to need to promote and market your book, if you want to get the most acclaim and financial return on investment. No exceptions.

No matter how much your Publishing company (vanity or otherwise) helps. Later on we'll finish with tips on how to deal with various publishing companies, online and off – as well as how to easily and effectively promote your book. (Don't worry – this report will help take multiple learning curves out of the process for you, as well as help you avoid mistakes and make the right choices.)

For now, however, let's take a look at the various options open to you as a Self-Publisher…

1. Information Products

This is the ultimate DIY method for Self-publishing, and if you have even a modicum of talent or skill in certain areas, you can produce one on an absolute, shoestring budget.

Also, if you are planning to use PLR[1] material to quickly create your book and get it out there on your own site, you are your own

Ultimate Boss: You don't have to worry about having your book "yanked" by Marketplaces such as Kindle (which absolutely vetoes PLR-based books).

Whenever you consider a Publishing method, always start by considering your market – the people who will eagerly pay to read your book.

So what do people who buy information products typically want from an information product author?

---

[1] *Private Label Rights* – generic content on a subject meant to be customized and altered to reflect your own persona and market slant

These are the top five responses:

1. Learn "how to" master something, do something, work something or create something

2. Learn quickly

3. Fill in "blanks" in a learning process

4. Save time and "shortcut" the learning process

5. Make money fast

Think about the reasons why you buy information products, yourself... why you bought this one, for example. How many of the previous five motives spurred your decision?

But producing information products independently brings with it a whole set of skills and components on top of all the other Self- publishing areas you have to consider: In addition to finding your unique book angle and providing high-quality information, setting up a marketing and promotion plan and actually writing your book, putting it into .PDF format and deciding if this is the best delivery system, you need to provide:

- **A dedicated website** (preferably a blog) for your Book

- **A landing page** for your Sales Letter

- **A "Thank you" page**

- A "Download" page
- A "Sign-up" page[1]

- **A professional-quality eCover** that reflects your book's most appealing message (and is relevant to the content!)

- **A system to accept payments**

- **A customer service system**, to process refunds, solve download glitches and answer questions

- **An Affiliate "Center"** (resource and information page and section), if you're planning to use affiliates or JV partners to help spread the word about your book

- **Resources for your Affiliates to use**

- **A system for Affiliate Payment** – you'll need to make sure your affiliates are properly and promptly rewarded!

- **A schedule or calendar** for all your processes – as well as your promotional endeavors

- **A database of names and numbers** – reviewers who have reviewed your book; newspaper and magazine

---

[1] Can be er

editors to send press releases to; readers supplying testimonials, and so forth.

(This database will become priceless in future promotional efforts for future books.)

- **Press releases**
- **A Newsletter**
- **A Facebook, Google and/or LinkedIn Business Page**
- **A Social Networking plan**
- **An Autoresponder**

You can also use your website and landing page as a sales aid, rather than as your main selling portal, if you use a marketplace such as ClickBank.

Your cost will be whatever your website and domain registration fees will be (choose a domain host that includes registration of one domain with your new account). Plus $49.50 to sign up as a Vendor with ClickBank. And the cost of whatever work you outsource (i.e. your blog set-up or graphic design for your header or PLR articles written for your affiliates, et cetera.)

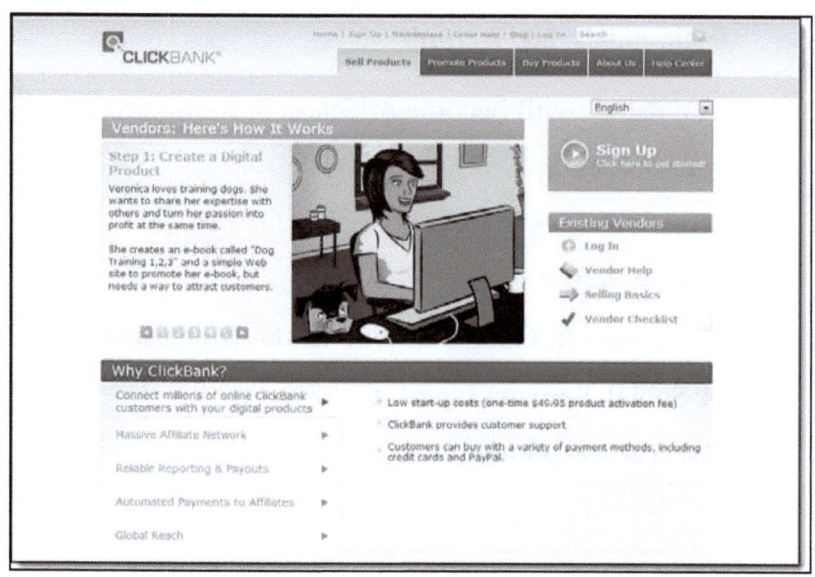

ClickBank has its quirks, so do be sure to read all its tutorials and Help section thoroughly. Its advantages? A wide reach; it supplies you with a "shopping cart" and takes care automatically of paying your affiliates, once you've set your commission.

Important points to remember with ClickBank:

1. Use your website ONLY FOR PROMOTION – do NOT put up a Sales page! Let ClickBank itself be your only sales portal. (The reason? Seasoned affiliates – that small percentage who will bring you the bulk of your

sales – will not invest time and effort in a product that is being sold elsewhere. This undercuts and sabotages their efforts.

2. Offer a high commission – at least 75%. You'll be making a minimal amount on your sales but will be planting strong seeds in the leads you generate and the buzz that gets spread.

3. Provide top quality resources for your affiliates

4. Be sure to choose the right category for your book

5. Provide your affiliates with instructions on how to cloak links, if you know better ways to do so than provided by ClickBank. (There are many link-cloaking methods, scripts and programs.) Encourage your affiliates to cloak their links, since it is unfortunately quite easy for others to change the links and steal their commissions.

6. Build your list *before* you put your book on ClickBank. (Use your Autoresponder to create a sign-up Web Form and offer a freebie – e.g. a chapter of your book.) That

way, you may line up quality affiliates before ever uploading your book.

7. Build a relationship with your affiliates. That way, they'll actually (a) remember who you are and (b) care about your sales. Send out an affiliates newsletter. Use contests for the most sales with a reward (cash is *always* welcome.)

8. Do your homework with ClickBank: Make sure there is a demand on that marketplace for your topic and be sure to upload it to the right category, using the right keywords.

9. Consider boosting your eBook sales with (free) DigiResults and PayDotCom . Many people report better success for eBooks when they integrate their ClickBank sales with these two particular online marketplaces

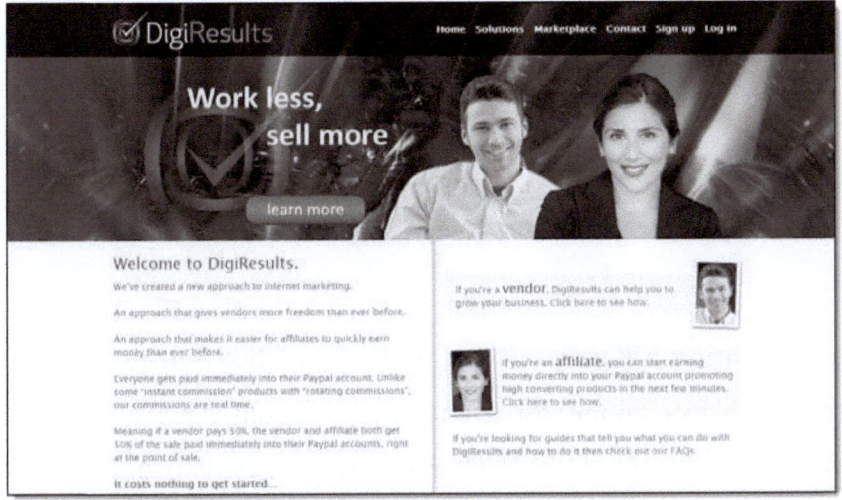

So there's more work than you thought selling information products directly; or through a marketplace such as ClickBank. Here's a way to make the process even simpler, cheaper and easier...

Kindle eBooks

Creating a Kindle eBook is the latest hot Self-publishing trend. Always taking for granted you should have a blog or website to promote your business, your biggest expense should be your Kindle eBook **eCover creation**.

When creating an eCover for Kindle, make sure that (a) Your illustration is in black-and-white (Kindle doesn't do color yet) and (b) it's professional, relevant and eye-catching – made by someone who understands the Kindle marketplace. (eCover creation can range anywhere from twenty dollars to three hundred and twenty, depending on how important you think your cover should be and which artist or graphics package you choose.)

You now have three Self-publishing options, when building your eBook for Kindle:

- Do-It-Yourself

- Print and Digital Option (CreateSpace, which we briefly touched on earlier in this Report)

- Using a professional Conversion Service

In other words, there's a Kindle Self-publishing process to suit every budget and marketing plan.

a) **Do-It-Yourself** – Your best bet, when putting a Kindle eBook together from scratch, is to go directly to their "Building Your eBook for Kindle" section and carefully read through it, as well as watching the tutorial slide show with audio:

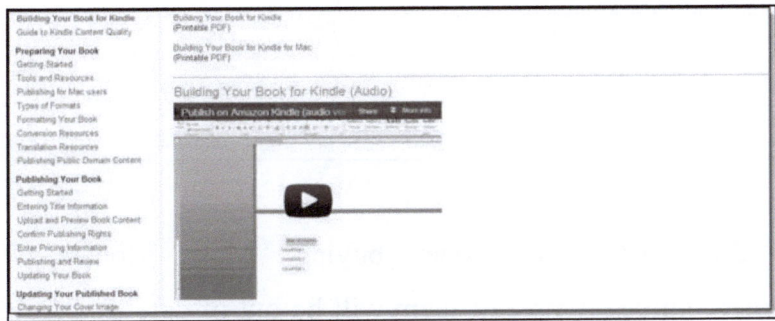

(There's also a **text-based slide show tutorial**.)

You can also download a .PDF version of all instructions. Kindle provides separate .PDFs for:

- MAC

- PC

Be sure also to work your way through the various sections in the left-hand sidebar menu: These cover everything you need to know from conversion resources to notifying customers about book updates.

On this page you will also find **the latest Kindle news and updates**.

So don't waste money buying "Make Money With Kindle!" guides – most of them will be out of date by the time you download them – and many contain tactics and strategies that not only violate or dangerously stretch Amazon Kindle's terms of service, but don't support long-term reputation building. They are "grab-the-cash- and-run" strategies.

When Should You Use Kindle? - Kindle is an ideal choice if your market is already made up of active Kindle users.

How can you tell? Simply load up Amazon's Kindle book catalogue. You'll instantly see which books are best sellers and what categories they come from. These are today's "hot" categories, so if your book fits one of them, you should definitely consider writing a Kindle eBook.

In addition, you'll find more Categories in the left-hand vertical menu. Click on any Category that interests you, and you'll find it will open up into a new page showing:

a) Another left-hand vertical menu listing highly specific Sub- Categories within the Category you selected

b) Current best sellers in your Category and which Sub-Category they came from

These are your biggest clues as to whether or not there is an audience for your book among Kindle's readership.

Other reasons to Self-Publish on Kindle include:

- If you wish to produce an Audio book. Kindle is thoroughly compatible with Audio book formats created in ACX

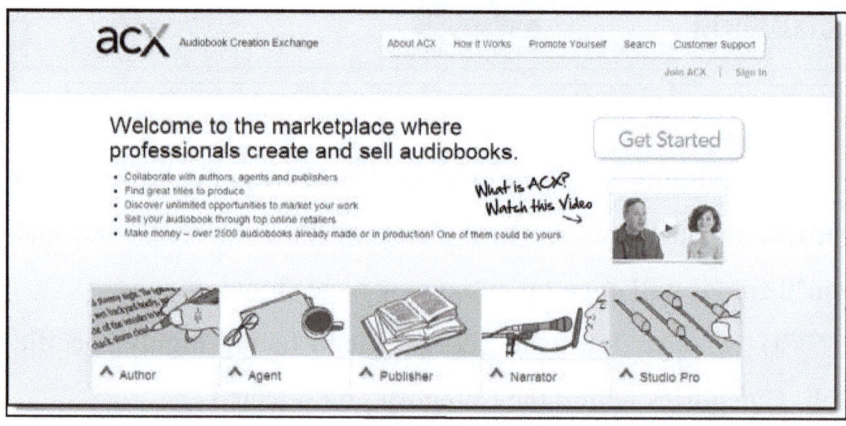

- When you'd like to publish your book in both Kindle Reader format and digital "on demand" printed format (using CreateSpace)[1]

- When you want to publish Public Domain content. (Kindle allows this, though it does not allow PLR content: However, they do have specific conditions so check out their Public Domain page.)

Kindle is ideal for the new author: They provide multiple tools, tips and resources (such as "Tax Information for non-US publishers" and "Changing your Cover Image").

But what if you want to Self-Publish your eBook in CD or DVD format?

---

[1] N.B. People will not be able to upgrade to a print copy if they are accessing your book through the Kindle Lending Library or KDP Direct.

Books on CD/DVD

You have a variety of options for product fulfillment, when it comes to putting your book on CD/DVD. These are good for very small orders and fulfillment-on-demand.

One of the most popular CD/DVD Self-publishing companies is Kunaki. Their website is off-puttingly barebones (without even a graphic) but their quality is consistently "good" to "high" and their delivery record excellent.

If you squinch your eyes up, you'll see the price of $1.00 given on their home page: Count on more like $5, when the dust has settled.

You download a piece of simple, dependable software on your desktop and a wizard walks you through setting up your eBook and choosing a Cover Graphic. (The print quality on their covers is excellent.) And if you create your product using Kunaki's software, you can have a Kunaki UPC bar code stamped on your jewel case (or use your own, if you have one to upload).

You can then sell your CD on Amazon in yet another format (CD/DVD). Multiple formats can increase your sale-ability, as well as the number of marketplaces and Categories your book is listed in, when it comes to Amazon.

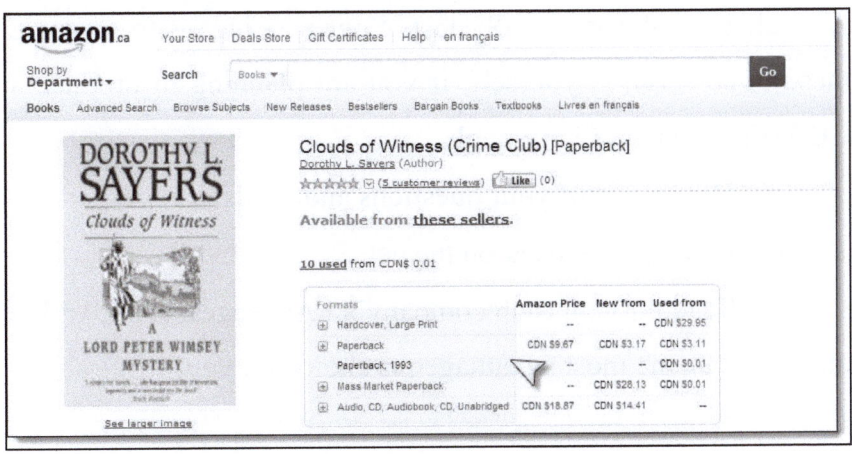

Kunaki drop-ships your CDs directly to Amazon. You can also have Kunaki ship large bulk orders to you… or ship directly to clients on a "per demand" basis.

Lately, however, Vervanté has been giving Kunaki a run for their money. Their quality is as good as Kunaki's if not better; and on sign-up for their freebie report, you get a twenty-five-percent discount coupon for your first order. And – unlike Kunaki – they allow additional printed inserts generated by you.

Vervanté is admittedly the most expensive but sometimes you can't judge solely by the dollar figure: Customer service is top-notch from Vervanté and they will ship anywhere in the world – quickly. (That includes shipment to military FPO/APO addresses).

Kunaki can take up to three weeks to ship to Canada, yet Australians report it is really fast. Your best idea is to compare these three services yourself, if you are planning to produce a CD/DVD version of your book.

- Make a list of your questions and needs
- Look up feedback on the net
- Read through each company's FAQ pages, to see which one would be the most advantageous choice for you.

Per Demand Product Fulfillment for Print Books

Of course, the disadvantage of Kunaki is that it doesn't provide print versions of your book to sell as alternatives (or with) your CDs.

Vervanté, on the other hand, does offer this option. Another time-honored Self-publishing company is Lulu...

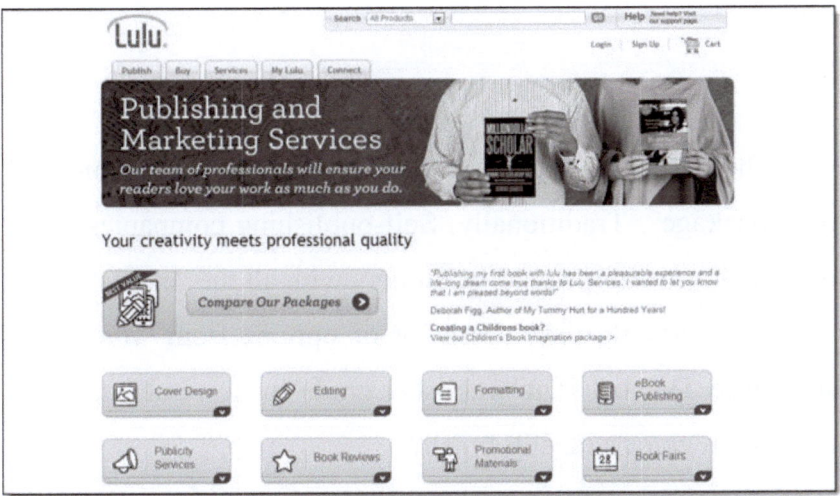

You can present your book in both eBook format and hard copy, to give your reader more individual choice.

And you can include illustrations and original artwork. You can calendars and "photo books". As well as both Manga comics and traditional cartoon- based books.

Where you have to be careful with Lulu lies in picking your "package". Traditionally, Self-publishing companies were notorious for nailing would-be authors with all the "extras".

Lulu certainly provides a lot of options from which you can choose. Do you want "publisher grade" paper, Lulu standard or premium grade with silk finish?

Full color… or high-quality black and white?

Pocket book size... or Crown Quarto? Saddle stitch... or Coil bound?

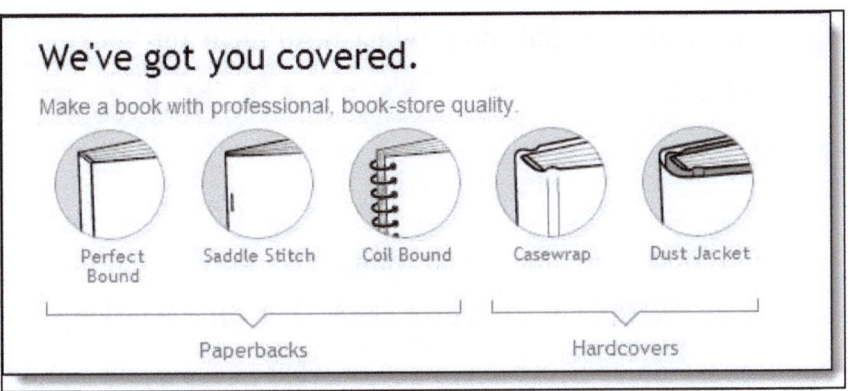

Lulu does provide a "cost-calculator" app in its left-hand Sidebar menu. And in case that's still too confusing, you can shortcut right to three package deals Lulu offers:

- **Best Seller** ($729.00)
- **Masterpiece** ($1,649.00)
- **Laureate** ($4,949.00)

Each package offers selected A-Z options, culminating in the Laureate package including full professional copy edit, 100 paperbacks and 25 hard covers. (All packages include an "Editorial Quality Review".)

> **Q**: "Does Lulu.com still do product fulfillment for books on CD/DVD?:"
>
> **A:** No.

Lulu does provide a full range of professional-quality services for everything you'll ever need – but when checking out your options, do consider that much of what you see you can do yourself, easily, using Amazon's services such as Kindle formatting and CreateSpace.

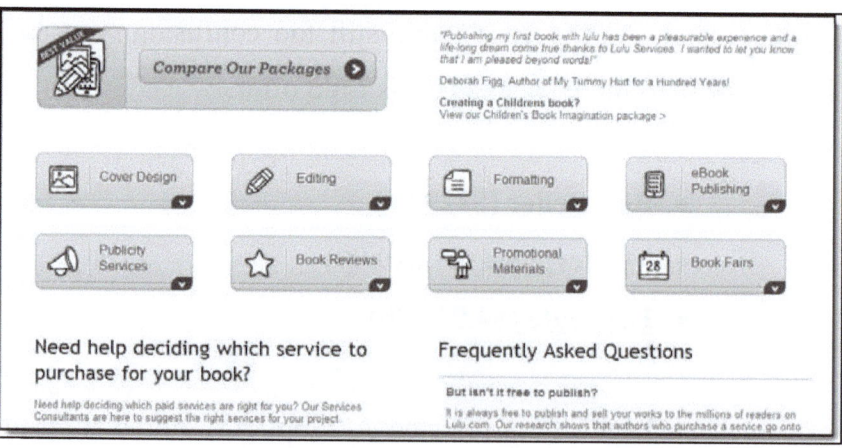

CreateSpace

And now we come to one of the easiest ways to Self-Publish you'll ever encounter -- CreateSpace, a company actually owned by Amazon.

It's a true "on demand" service; meaning that if no one orders, you don't pay. It is, however, a royalty-based system – which works well in your favor if you make heavy sales; and not at all if you only make one or two, here and there. And you can order multiples of books to distribute yourself.

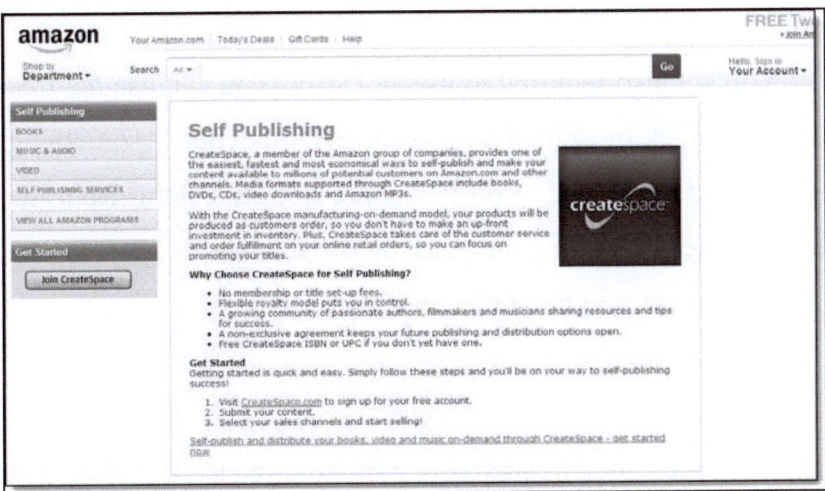

You can do all the work yourself (with the assistance of CreateSpace's well-designed, easy-to-use tools)... or you can opt for a Self-publishing services "plan" (package deal on service) – in effect, outsourcing all your file creation to CreateSpace itself.

If you do opt for the free "do-it-yourself" route, note that you *will* have to pay for a "proof copy" and review your book to ensure it is publishing- ready. If you're careful, you can get away with one proof copy, but most people seem to find they run to four or five.

This should hardly break your bank, however: Proof copies usually cost slightly more or less than ***ten to fifteen dollars per copy***.

You are also required to use an ISBN. You can use the free ISBN provided, or upload your own ISBN barcode – something you may actually need to do if you are not publishing from the United States.[1] (Putting in your own bar code is easy to do: Simply enter it into your Title Set-up.)

---

[1] Canadians can register themselves as publishers with the Canadian ISBN Service HSystem
(CISS) from Library and Archives Canada, to be eligible for free ISBNs.

One of CreateSpace's biggest advantages? It has it all right there in one Self-publishing venue. You can create:

- Books
- Video DVDs
- Audio CDs and MP3s
- Music CDs

One great feature of CreateSpace: Its "Interior Reviewer", which allows you to see what your book will truly look like in its finished form before you've released it. Interior Reviewer provides a great way to catch errors and check formatting: It even points errors out to you, in a visually easy- to-understand way.

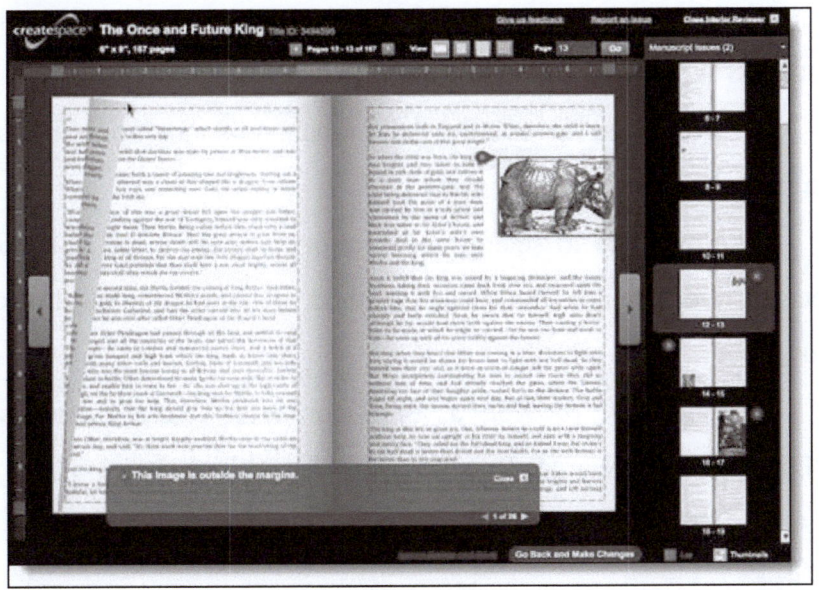

"Is CreateSpace free?" – It can be. Almost.

And it will place your book on Amazon for free: As well as send you a fat booklet containing *"555 Tips for Improving Your Book Promotion"* if you request a free consultation; in which they'll pitch what they can do for you, if you choose a services package. (*"Choose from a full array of editing, book design, and marketing services to meet your needs and budget"*…)

CreateSpace Disadvantages – While this Self-publishing program is the easiest to use in many ways, it does have some glitchy features and disadvantages:

- You may have problems with picture compression, if your MS Word program is not up-to-date

- You need to ensure that Amazon is not applying a surcharge to your book per copy

- You have to set up an account in order to be able to access Cover Creator (the easiest method of setting up your book Cover)

- Does not provide a .PDF converter – but demands .PDFs for multiple areas (e.g. your Cover graphic)

- If you are living outside of the United States, CreateSpace withholds thirty percent of your Royalties for taxes. And you have to get a tax number.

MJ Preston explains this issue succinctly during an excellent Motley Press comparison of CreateSpace vs. Lulu…

Taxes and the IRS

If you are a not a US citizen, like me, there is also the tax issue to consider. Createspace withholds 30% of your revenue for the IRS and the only way to avoid this is to apply for an Individual Tax Identification Number (ITIN). Getting an ITIN requires you make an application to the IRS, along with this you are required to get a document notarized to prove who you are. If you are Canadian you'll have to cross the border because the IRS doesn't recognize Canadian Notary's.

On the other hand, Lulu gives you all your royalty money and says, "You pay the taxes." No IRS, no notary to deal with and no withholding percentages. Great, but then the taxman in your Country will still be waiting for their cut at the end of the filing year.

CreateSpace Advantages – One of CreateSpace's best resources is its professionally-run Forum. Not only can you get immediate, helpful feedback from other Self-Publishers who are one or more steps ahead of you, but here's where you can instantly see if there any changes to CreateSpace.

While other people are accessing blogs (and trying to remember which web page or site to go to) to get news about the services, social networks or programs they are using, CreateSpace's Forum provides access to just about every service, answer or resource automatically right there, in one spot.

All you have to do is look at the your screen…

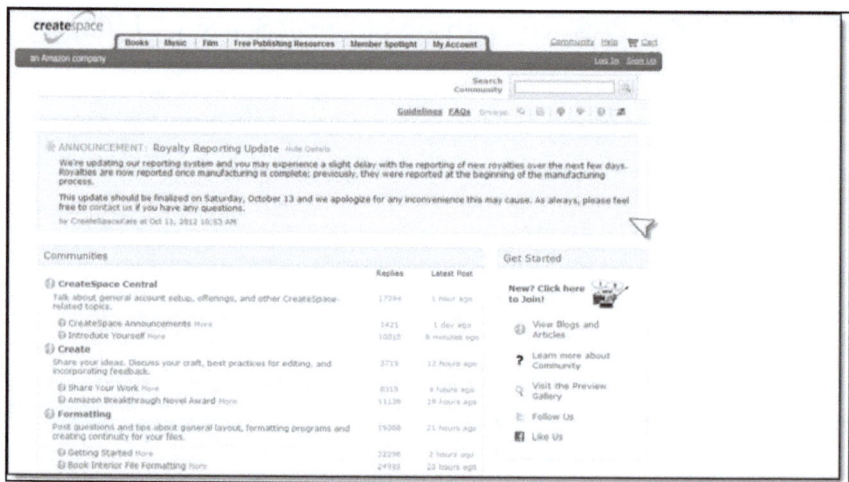

Notice in the right-hand bottom "Get Started" Sidebar vertical menu, there are also link to other resources and options. Plus the FAQs tab answers common questions such as "I forgot my account password" and "What are profile tabs?"

And don't forget to make full use of the Forum's "Free Publishing Resources" tab:

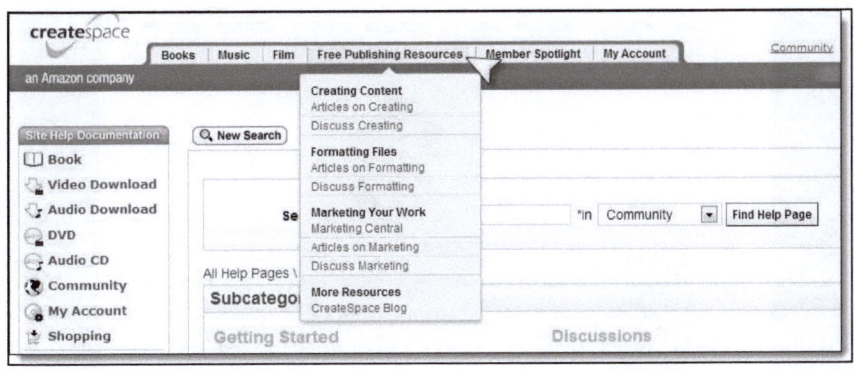

Also, CreateSpace consistently checks out as your most inexpensive option: Whether or not you are opting for one of their "plans" or paying stand-alone prices.

"But What if I'm Producing a Manga or Comic Book?" – If your novel is any sort of Graphic novel and you are new to Self-publishing, you'll absolutely want to check out Indie-publisher, Ka-blam.

You can reduce your printing costs even further by allowing Ka-Blam to place a full-Page ad at the back of your comic or Manga.

As for ease of use, this is what Emily Ragozzino, creator of *"Why I Hate Cheerleaders"* had to say, in discussing why after several titles she later switched from Lulu to Ka-Blam:

"Lulu works ok but I found the formatting difficult to do on there. It took me a while to figure it out and I was all self-taught. I'm not sure I did it all right on there to this day, I think I published it in the easiest method I could figure out. I'm still on

Lulu for Dork Girl and Why I Hate Cheerleaders and it's cool that people can download my book for a small fee or buy it hard copy if they want it but the marketing isn't that amazing on there. It's all up to the creator to market it, which is the hard part about self publishing.

They did put my stuff on Amazon.ca for a while, which is cool, but because the books weren't moving well I think they took them off of there. I ended up switching over to try Ka-Blam as they're a more comic based
Indie company and I was really happy with the quality of it for my Tom Boy Tara books. Again, my marketing for the books suck, I only seem to move the books when I'm at comic stores or conventions and pushing them on people."

Ragozzino brings up an important point...

Marketing Your Book as a Self-Publisher

You can't escape it. No matter how much you outsource, no matter what Self-publishing company, method or system you use, your book sales won't reach their maximum potential until you actively begin helping with promotion and marketing.

This means:

- Creating a Facebook Page for your book[1]

- Using other Social Media where your audience can be found (E.G. a Google Plus Page, if you're a restaurant publishing a book of recipes; A Twitter presence, if your audience is most active there; A LinkedIn Page, if your book is all about business issues)

- Doing book signings at libraries and book stores, if you are placing hardcovers or paperbacks in the "real world"

---

[1] This is a "must", crossing all social preferences

- Maintaining a blog and allowing people to get to know you and identify with you

- Making people care about your book

- Making sure you learn how to share a chapter or so on Amazon. (Nothing puts people off more than not being able to look inside an unknown new author's book – especially if yours has a high price point: I.E. over $2.99.)

- Marketing your book in multiple formats, across multiple venues

- Doing radio or local TV interviews

(Unlike comedienne Kathy Griffin, however, you can stop short of falling dramatically out of taxis for the camera – one of her most famous publicity stunts.)

When you think of it, active promotion is not only an inevitable part of the process, but simply common sense.

Or, in metaphysical terms, if you pour energy into something, that will generate energy.

"Which Option is Best – and Most Easy -- For Me?"

As you have seen from hitting the highs and lows of various Self-publishing systems and services, there is no one definitive answer. You'll find authors raving and cursing about every system or method.

There's always a learning curve. You will always make mistakes or need help on some "sticky" spot (unless you pay top dollar and outsource the lot; in which case, if you don't do your homework properly, you risk getting ripped off in the time-dishonored method of the old-style Vanity publisher).

And there are always "hidden" costs. (Translation: Every task you let the Self-publishing company do for you will cost ya.)

Doing it yourself (and maybe outsourcing only specific tasks you find particularly disagreeable or difficult) seems to be – believe it or not – the easiest way to go: A cost-effective compromise.

But do your homework: When you are considering a Self-publishing company, at the very least, Google your prospective business partner specifically to see what the **complaints** – and **benefits** – are (remembering that what's a complaint to one person might be a benefit to you; or vice-versa).

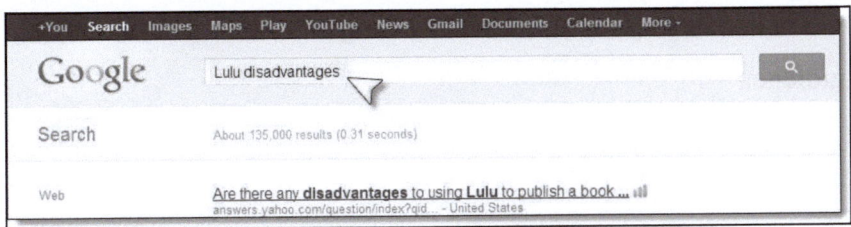

Find their **Forums**, if they have one. See what problems and issues members are having in real-time – and particularly look for how easy it is to solve these: And whether or not it is an active user community, with helpful "super members".

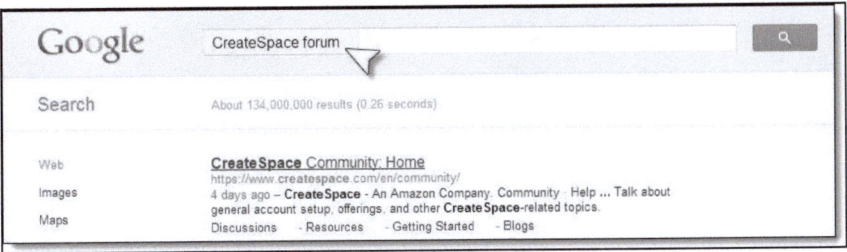

The real key to Self-publishing success lies in taking time to check out and find the system that will:

a) Give you the best ROI

b) Feel the most comfortable to work with

c) Best fit your budget

d) Provide the resources you need

e) Allow you to connect with your most active, buying audience

9 786069 837313

Printed by Libri Plureos GmbH in Hamburg, Germany